**PEGASUS ENCYCLOPEDIA LIBRARY**

# Food and Nutrition
# DIET AND RECIPES

Edited by: Pallabi B. Tomar, Hitesh Iplani
Managing editor: Tapasi De
Designed by: Vijesh Chahal, Anil Kumar, Rohit Kumar
Illustrated by: Suman S. Roy, Tanoy Choudhury
Colouring done by: Vinay Kumar, Kiran Kumari & Pradeep Kumar

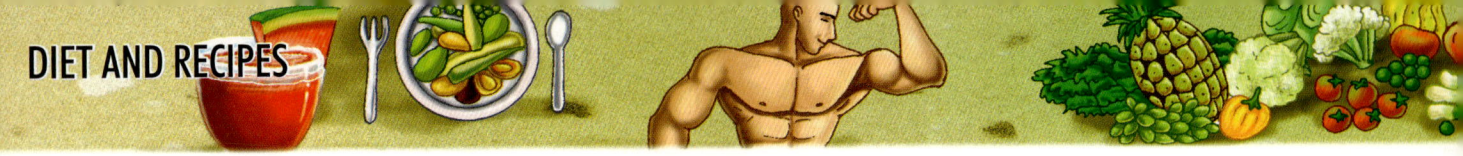

# CONTENTS

Introduction ............................................................. 3

Balanced diet .......................................................... 5

Types of diets .......................................................... 7

Body mass index .................................................... 11

Importance of diet ................................................. 13

Role of nutrients .................................................... 15

Diet according to body types ................................ 18

Some healthy recipes ............................................ 21

Test Your Memory ................................................. 31

Index ....................................................................... 32

# Introduction

Diet is the sum of food consumed by a person or other living being. The human body is a large and complicated organism. There are many different parts of the body that perform several unique functions. Different organ systems perform automatic tasks that help maintain the life of the body. This complicated nature of the human body means that its dietary requirements are equally complicated. A healthy diet is therefore one that contains all the necessary nutrients in appropriate amounts. The dietary requirement of every human being is different from every other human being. Some individuals are more athletic and spend more energy while others are more relaxed and tend not to spend too much time on physical pursuits. The profession of an individual is also important when it comes to a balanced diet. Some individuals' work involves intense physical labour, while others sit at desks all day and do not expend much physical energy. Instead, these people spend their energy on mental tasks. Therefore, a lumberjack working in a forest requires a different diet from that of an IT professional working in an office.

In general, raw vegetables have a much higher nutrient value than cooked, though there are a few exceptions, such as cooked tomatoes.

# DIET AND RECIPES

The human body requires food to provide energy for all life process and for growth, repair and maintenance of cells and tissues. The dietetic needs vary according to age, sex and occupation. A balanced diet contains different types of foods in such quantities and proportions that the need for calories, minerals, vitamins and other nutrients is adequately met. A small provision is also made of extra nutrients which the body might need to fall back on short periods of leanness. Eating a well balanced diet on a regular basis and maintaining your ideal weight are critical factors in maintaining your emotional and physical well-being. Being over weight/under weight can lead to certain chronic conditions such as diabetes, high blood pressure and heart disease.

Fluid intake in the form of water based drinks is also essential for good health. Water is essential for the correct functioning of the kidneys and bowels. At least 6-8 glasses of plain water should be drunk each day, more in hot weather.

## Astonishing fact

Green fruits are the most vital of all fruits since they contain a chemical that protects you against heart attack and keeps your heart healthy.

# Balanced diet

A balanced diet is one that has all the essential nutrients, required by the body for proper growth and development, in the appropriate amounts. A well balanced diet consists of the right amounts of carbohydrates, proteins, fats, vitamins and minerals. A balanced diet also provides the body energy to function.

A balanced diet is one that features foods from all the important food groups that are used by the human body. These food groups include **protein** which is used to build body tissue, **carbohydrates** that are used for energy, **vitamins** and **minerals** that are used for various important body functions, **fat** that is used for energy storage and dietary fibre which helps the process of digestion.

When choosing a healthy diet, one should focus on naturally occurring foods rather than processed foods. All natural foods have varied nutritional qualities. Processed foods maybe rich in certain nutrients, but may fall short in other areas. A natural food based diet is one that can be a healthy diet and a balanced diet as well. A good, nutritious diet is essential for the proper functioning of the body and the proper functioning of the mind as well. When the body is in harmony, the individual can perform his or her daily tasks more efficiently.

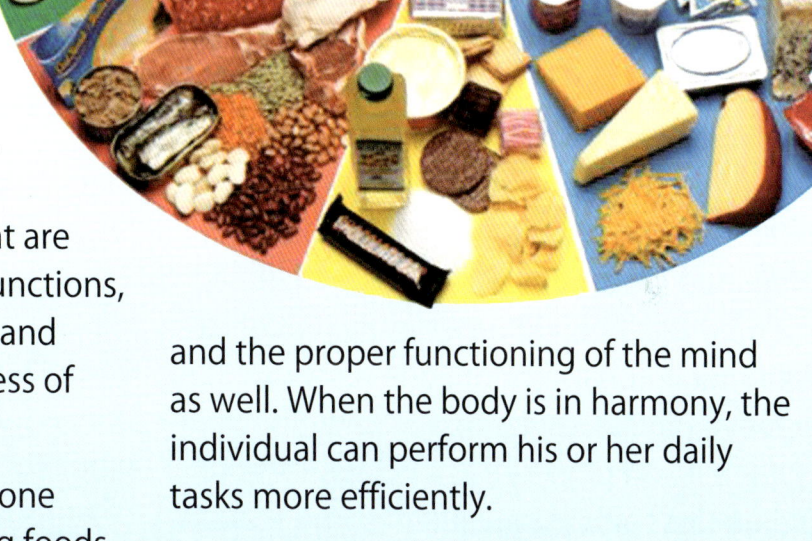

The mega-sized apples and oranges seen at grocers are pumped up due to added water volume, rather than fruit substance. This is a crop-yield technique used by farmers designed to produce bigger fruit for more consumer appeal.

# DIET AND RECIPES

When it comes to a diet for weight loss, one should understand that there are two areas of focus. Firstly, weight loss is related to the amount of exercise that an individual does. During exercise, food and then fat is burned for energy. By reducing one's food consumption, one will only achieve partial results. Starving the body is not a good plan as this causes sudden weight loss and may result in some sort of toxicity within the body, especially if there is no balance in the system. The second aspect of a diet for weight loss is the quantity and quality of food that is consumed. Once an individual has a set exercise regime, the diet can be modified accordingly. Individuals should eat meals at a set time and should avoid irregular snacking. Exercise should be done in an empty stomach so that the body needs to access fat for energy much faster than it would on a full stomach. An extensive use of fruits and vegetables is recommended.

A diet for weight loss and muscle gain is based on higher protein than a normal healthy diet. This is because protein is the raw material that is used to build muscle tissue.

> **Astonishing fact**
>
> The flavour of bubble gum comes from the fusion of vanilla, wintergreen and 'cassia,' a form of cinnamon.

# Types of diets

## Fixed-menu diet

A fixed-menu diet provides a list of all the foods you will eat. This kind of diet can be easy to follow because the foods are selected for you. But you get very few different food choices which may make the diet boring and hard to follow. In addition, fixed-menu diets do not teach the food selection skills necessary for keeping weight off. If you start with a fixed-menu diet, you should switch eventually to a plan that helps you learn to make meal choices on your own, such as an exchange-type diet.

## Exchange-type diet

An exchange-type diet is a meal plan with a set number of servings from each of several food groups. Within each group, foods are about equal in calories and can be interchanged as you wish. For example,

the 'starch' category could include one slice of bread or 1/2 cup of oatmeal; each is about equal in nutritional value and calories. If your meal plan calls for two starch choices at breakfast, you could choose to eat two slices of bread, or one slice of bread and 1/2 cup of oatmeal. With the exchange-type diet plans, you have more day-to-day variety and you can easily follow the diet away from home. The most important advantage is that exchange-type diet plans teach the food selection skills you need to keep your weight off.

### Astonishing fact

There is evidence that honey is the only food that does not spoil at all. Archaeologists have tasted honey discovered in ancient Egyptian tombs, reporting that it was still edible!

# DIET AND RECIPES

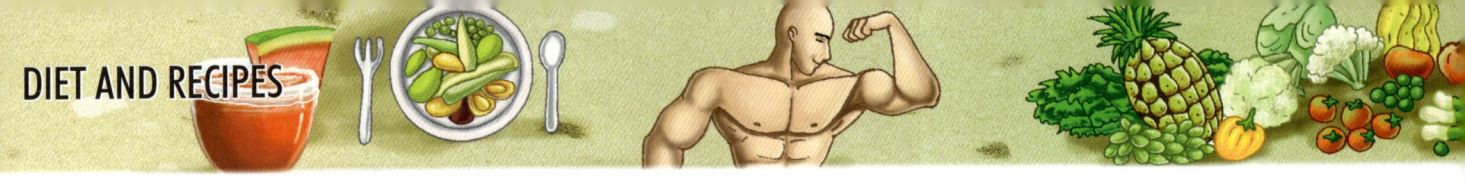

## Formula diet

Formula diets are weight-loss plans that replace one or more meals with a liquid formula. Most formula diets are balanced diets containing a mix of protein, carbohydrate and usually a small amount of fat. Formula diets are usually sold as liquid or a powder to be mixed with liquid. Although formula diets are easy to use and do promote short-term weight loss, most people regain the weight as soon as they stop using the formula. In addition, formula diets do not teach you how to make healthy food choices, a necessary skill for keeping your weight off.

## Pre-packaged meal diet

These diets require you to buy pre-packaged meals. Such meals may help you learn appropriate portion sizes. However, they can be costly. Before beginning this type of program, find out whether you need to buy the meals or not and how much the meals would cost you. You should also find out whether the program will teach you how to select and prepare food, skills that are needed to sustain weight loss.

## Astonishing fact

Popcorn have existed for around 6,000 years!

# Types of diets

## Questionable diets

You should avoid any diet that suggests you to eat a certain nutrient, food or combination of foods to promote easy weight loss. Some of these diets may work in the short term because they are low in calories. However, they are often not well balanced and may cause nutrient deficiencies. In addition, they do not teach eating habits that are important for a long-term weight management.

## Flexible diets

Some programs or books suggest monitoring the fat only, calories only or a combination of the two, with the individual making the choice of both the type and amount of food eaten. This flexible type of approach works well for many people, and teach them how to control what they eat. One drawback of flexible diets is that some don't consider the total diet. For example, programs that monitor fat only often allow people to take in unlimited amounts of excess calories from sugars, and therefore don't lead to weight loss.

It is important to choose an eating plan that you can live with. The plan should also teach you how to select and prepare healthy foods, as well as how to maintain your new weight. Remember that many people tend to regain lost weight. Eating a healthful and nutritious diet to maintain your new weight, combined with regular physical activity, helps to prevent weight regain.

### Astonishing fact

There are 1,200 varieties of watermelon.

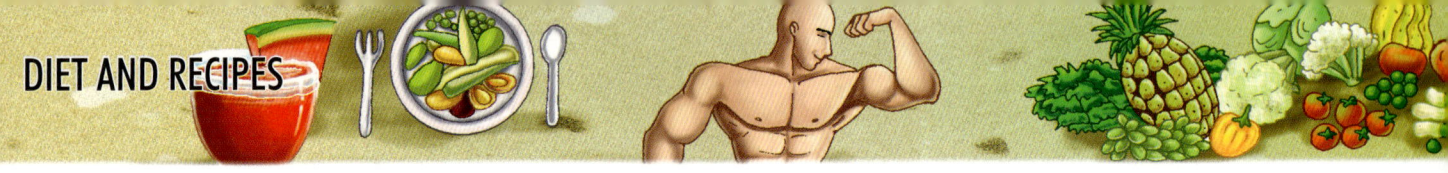

# DIET AND RECIPES

## Low-calorie diet

A low-calorie diet is a low-energy diet. The goal of a low-calorie diet is to create an energy deficit by providing fewer calories than your body needs so that the body has to draw upon the energy stored in body fat.

A low-calorie diet can be recognized by the types of foods recommended and the way they are prepared. Fresh fruits and vegetables, whole-grain cereals and breads, non-fat milk, yogurt, and other dairy products and lean meats, poultry, fish, and beans make up the bulk of the menu. Foods are prepared using low-calorie cooking methods. For example, meats, poultry and fish are roasted, baked or broiled, not fried. Vegetables are steamed, boiled or micro waved without using butter.

## Low-fat diet

A low-fat diet is made up primarily of foods that contain carbohydrates and fibre, including whole-grain breads and cereals, fruits, vegetables, and dried beans and peas. A low-fat diet should contain fewer foods from animal sources or should replace them with foods that are low in fat like low-fat milk and yogurt.

In addition, a low-fat diet should contain more foods from plant sources, which provide fibre, are low in saturated fat, and do not contain cholesterol. Lean meats, poultry, fish and low-fat or non-fat milk and yogurt supply protein.

### Astonishing fact

In order to have a therapeutic effect from green tea, you must consume 4-5 cups of it daily.

# Body mass index

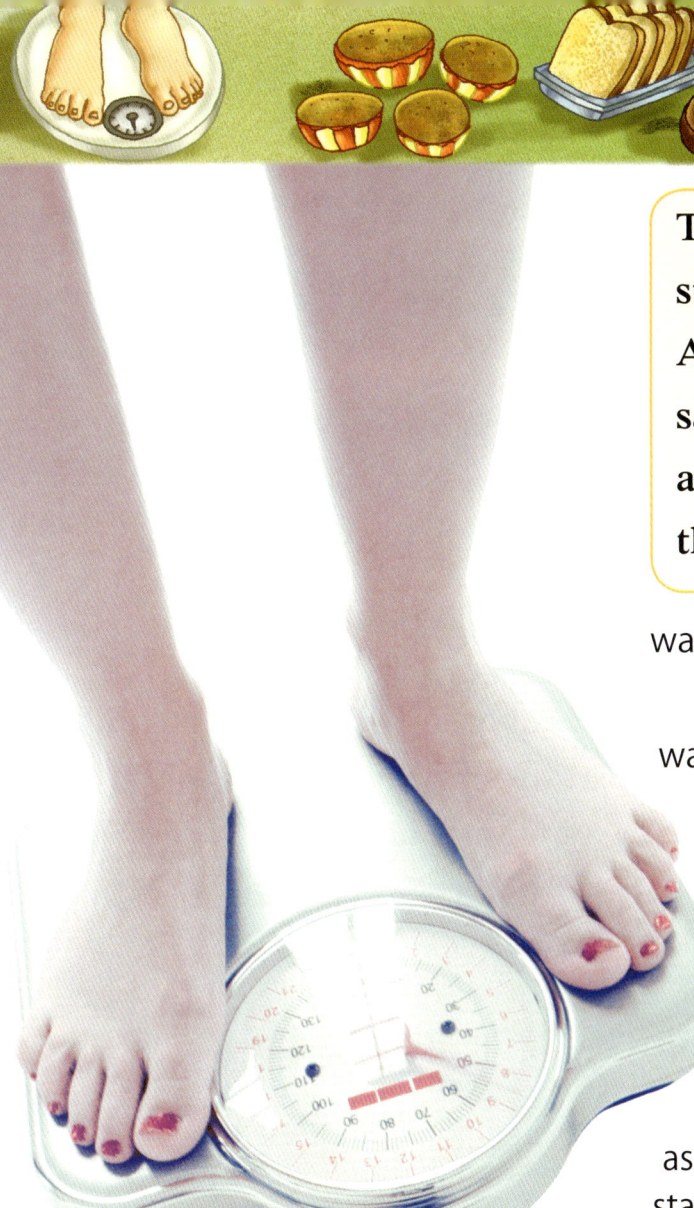

> The closer a food is to its natural state, the healthier it is for you. An apple is better than apple sauce which is better than bottled apple juice which is again better than apple pie.

way to check on how a kid is growing.

The Body mass index (BMI) formula was developed by Belgium statistician Adolphe Quetelet (1796-1874) and was known as the Quetelet Index. BMI is also referred to as 'body mass indicator'. BMI is an internationally used measure of obesity.

BMI has been used by the World Health Organisation (WHO) as the standard for recording obesity statistics since the early 1980s. In the United States, BMI is also used as a measure of underweight.

Body mass index (BMI) is a calculation that uses your height and weight to estimate how much body fat you have. Too much body fat is a problem because it can lead to illnesses and other health problems. BMI, although not a perfect method for judging someone's weight, is often a good

# DIET AND RECIPES

Body mass index calculation is very straightforward. Calculating body mass index requires only two measurements, height and weight.

The metric BMI formula accepts weight measurements in kilograms and height measurements in either centimetres or metres.

1 metre = 100 cms

metre² = metres × metres

Table: Metric BMI formula

$$\text{BMI (kg/m}^2\text{)} = \frac{\text{weight in kilograms}}{\text{height in metres}^2}$$

The formula is designed for adults over 20 years old. Once calculated, Body Mass Index can be compared to weight status categories to determine if an individual is:

- underweight (BMI: below 19.5)
- normal weight (BMI: 18.5 - 24.9)
- overweight (BMI: 25.0 to 29.9)
- obese (BMI: 30.0 & above)

> The reason some canned juices taste so good is because they contain a lot of sugar.

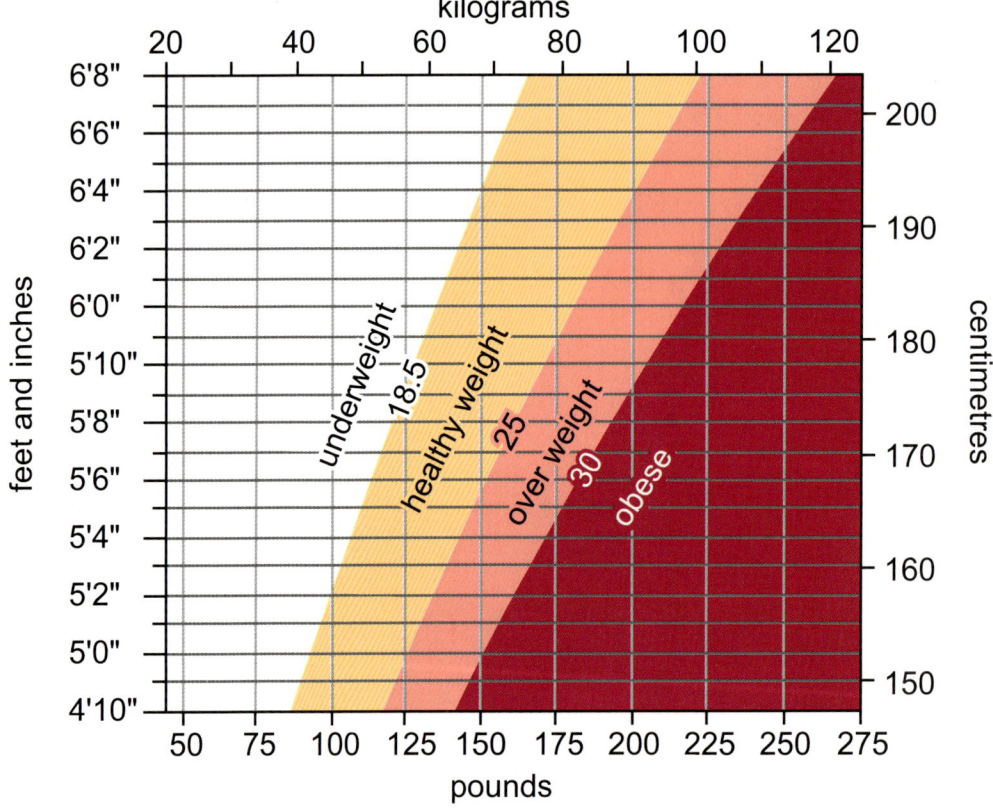

**Body Mass Index (BMI) for adults**

Source: National Institutes of Health/National Heart, Lung, and Blood Institute

# Importance of diet

Nowadays, there are many health problems that people are experiencing, which are arising due to several reasons. For most of the problems, the correct and only solution is a balanced diet. Many people have a misconception that a balanced diet means to avoid eating specific foodstuffs which may prove harmful to the body. It actually means to eat all types of food, but in a balanced amount which will provide all necessary nutrients to maintain a healthy body.

## Preventing infections and diseases

Eating all kinds of foods in a well-balanced proportion will help your body to prevent many infections and disorders. If the body gets all the required nutrients, it will improve the functioning of the immune system which is responsible for the prevention of various infections. By following a balanced diet, you reduce the possibilities of some types of cancer, control blood sugar levels effectively and control blood pressure also.

## Controlling weight

For the purpose of reducing and controlling weight, people tend to forget why a balanced diet is important. They don't understand that a balanced diet is the key to reduce or increase weight. Those who want to reduce weight try different ways, but don't succeed. The reason is that the routines they choose include consuming huge amounts of foods that don't contribute to weight loss.

### Astonishing fact

Bananas will never become brown, if you refrigerate them.

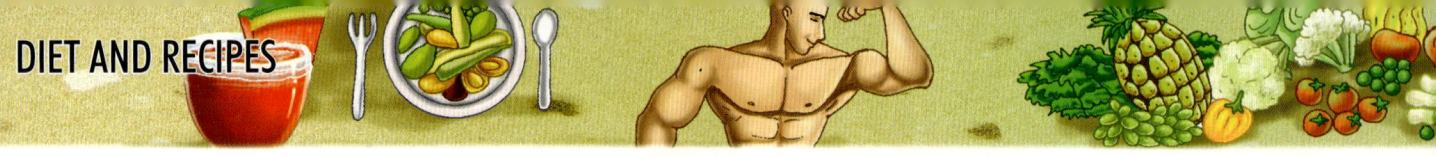

## Healthy growth of a body

If the body is getting all the essential nutrients regularly, it will certainly be fit. It would be away from infections and diseases, which in turn will promote a healthy body, growth and maintenance. A balanced diet should be implemented in the routine of a growing child or a teenager. You would be able to easily perform physical tasks without any exertion on the body. It is a necessity nowadays, as there is so much physical and mental stress in the lives of people.

## Active lifestyle

A balanced diet would also be beneficial to the state of mind. You would be able to live an active lifestyle. As both the body and mind would be in a good state, they would coordinate effectively. It will help you to take immediate decisions and tackle problems efficiently. It is also proven to increase the remembering and memorizing capability of a person.

There are many more advantages that a balanced diet has to offer. The chances of your body getting infected would be reduced considerably. It would also help you to stop the development and spreading of the diseases and infections which you are suffering from.

# Importance of diet

Nowadays, there are many health problems that people are experiencing, which are arising due to several reasons. For most of the problems, the correct and only solution is a balanced diet. Many people have a misconception that a balanced diet means to avoid eating specific foodstuffs which may prove harmful to the body. It actually means to eat all types of food, but in a balanced amount which will provide all necessary nutrients to maintain a healthy body.

## Preventing infections and diseases

Eating all kinds of foods in a well-balanced proportion will help your body to prevent many infections and disorders. If the body gets all the required nutrients, it will improve the functioning of the immune system which is responsible for the prevention of various infections. By following a balanced diet, you reduce the possibilities of some types of cancer, control blood sugar levels effectively and control blood pressure also.

## Controlling weight

For the purpose of reducing and controlling weight, people tend to forget why a balanced diet is important. They don't understand that a balanced diet is the key to reduce or increase weight. Those who want to reduce weight try different ways, but don't succeed. The reason is that the routines they choose include consuming huge amounts of foods that don't contribute to weight loss.

### Astonishing fact

Bananas will never become brown, if you refrigerate them.

# DIET AND RECIPES

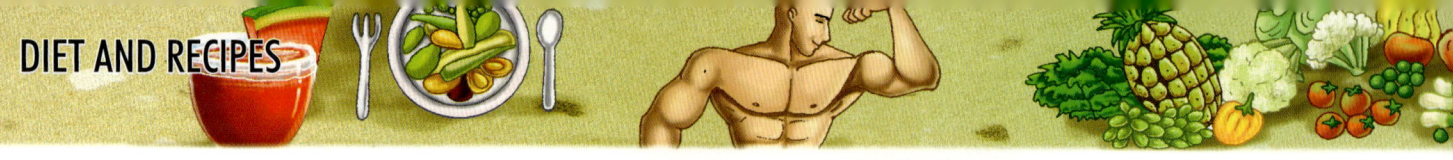

## Healthy growth of a body

If the body is getting all the essential nutrients regularly, it will certainly be fit. It would be away from infections and diseases, which in turn will promote a healthy body, growth and maintenance. A balanced diet should be implemented in the routine of a growing child or a teenager. You would be able to easily perform physical tasks without any exertion on the body. It is a necessity nowadays, as there is so much physical and mental stress in the lives of people.

## Active lifestyle

A balanced diet would also be beneficial to the state of mind. You would be able to live an active lifestyle. As both the body and mind would be in a good state, they would coordinate effectively. It will help you to take immediate decisions and tackle problems efficiently. It is also proven to increase the remembering and memorizing capability of a person.

There are many more advantages that a balanced diet has to offer. The chances of your body getting infected would be reduced considerably. It would also help you to stop the development and spreading of the diseases and infections which you are suffering from.

# Role of nutrients

Our body needs important nutrients to support its healthy condition. It is mandatory that our food consumption should include healthy foods that contain good amount of nutrients sufficient enough to supply our body with its required daily nutrition.

## Carbohydrates

Carbohydrates are the most important source of energy. They contain the elements carbon, hydrogen and oxygen. We obtain most of our carbohydrate in the form of starch. This is found in potato, rice, spaghetti, yams, bread and cereals. Our digestive system turns all this starch into another carbohydrate called **glucose**. Glucose is carried around the body in the blood and is used by our tissues as a source of energy. We also get some of our carbohydrate in the form of sucrose; this is the sugar which we put in our tea and coffee.

## Proteins

Proteins are required for growth and repair. Where carbohydrates and fats are broken down to produce energy, protein is broken down to give your body material for tissue repair and growth. Common protein rich foods may include milk, soy milk, eggs, cheese, yogurt, peanut butter, lean meats, fish and poultry, beans, tofu, lentils and other legumes, grains, including bread and pasta, nuts and seeds.

### Astonishing fact

Two 12-ounce servings of freshly juiced apples, pears, carrots, celery and leafy greens can produce the same effect as twice the dose of a laxative.

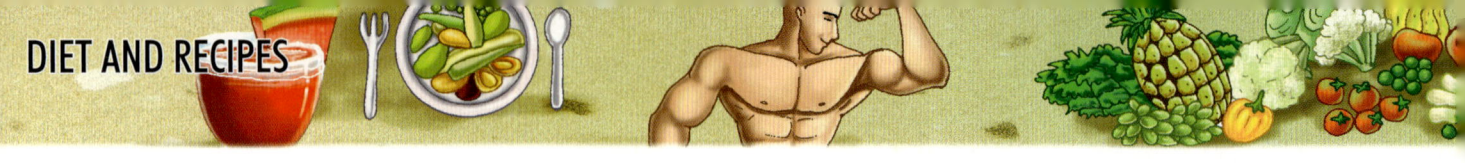

## Fats

Fats are our storehouses of energy. When we have excess nutrients in our body, some of it is stored as fat. The primary purpose of fat is energy production. There are two main types of fats— saturated and unsaturated. Animal fats (meat, butter, lard) are usually saturated fats and contribute to heart disease and cancer. Vegetable fats (olive oil, corn oil) are generally unsaturated fats and are less harmful.

## Vitamins

Vitamins are substances that your body needs to grow and develop normally. There are 13 vitamins your body needs. They are vitamins A, C, D, E, K and the B vitamins (thiamine, riboflavin, niacin, pantothenic acid, biotin, vitamin B-6, vitamin B-12 and folate). You can usually get all your vitamins from the foods you eat. Your body can also make vitamins D and K.

Each vitamin has specific jobs. If you have low levels of certain vitamins, you may develop a deficiency disease. For example, if you don't get enough vitamin D, you could develop rickets. Some vitamins may help prevent medical problems. Vitamin A prevents night blindness.

### Astonishing fact

Diet soda has not been proven to aid in weight loss. In fact, it's been shown to actually increase hunger!

# Role of nutrients

## Minerals

Minerals are compounds obtained from your diet that combine in several ways to form the structures of your body. For instance, calcium is a mineral that is crucial in the formation and maintenance of your bones. Minerals also help regulate body functions. Minerals do not produce energy.

## Water

Water is perhaps the most critical nutrient. We can live without other nutrients for several weeks, but we can go without water for only about one week. The body needs water to carry out all of its life processes. Watery solutions help dissolve other nutrients and carry them to all the tissues. The chemical reactions that turn food into energy or tissue-building materials can take place only in a watery solution. The body also needs water to carry away waste products and to cool itself.

Whenever a recipe for cake or muffins calls for oil, applesauce can be substituted in place of it.

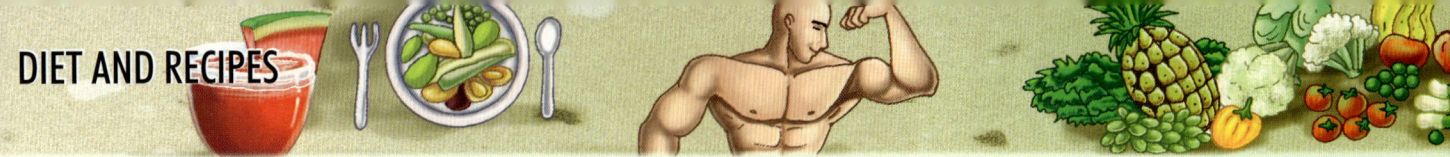

DIET AND RECIPES

# Diet according to body types

All people fall into three basic body types— ectomorph, mesomorph and endomorph. A body type diet suggests that we eat certain foods based on our body type, and that eating this way will help promote a proper weight and our overall health and well-being.

## Ectomorph body type diet

The ectomorph body type is naturally lean. If you are an ectomorph you will tend to be taller and tend to burn calories quickly. You may find it difficult to keep the weight on. This does not mean an ectomorph should indulge in greasy overly fatty foods. Doing so will only increase their risk of cardiovascular disease and high blood pressure, whether they are naturally lean or not. Rather an ectomorph should focus on eating multiple times per day and eating nutritious and calorie dense foods. Ample proteins, carbohydrates and fats should be included in the diet. Extra protein may help build more lean muscle.

### Astonishing fact

Apples are more efficient than coffee at keeping people awake in the morning.

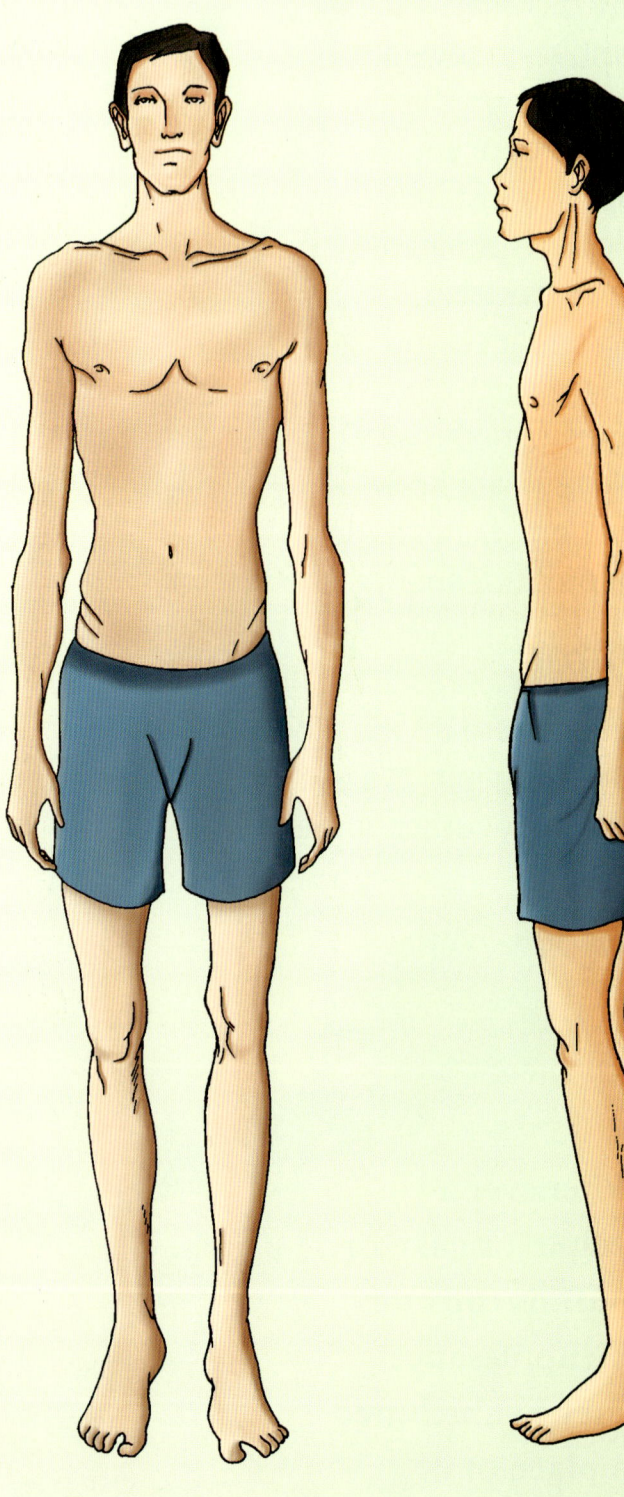

# Diet according to body types

## Mesomorph body type diet

People with a mesomorph body type have average builds with the muscle definition and strength of an athlete having broad shoulders and a narrow waist. Mesomorphs build muscle easily. A fast metabolism helps people with the mesomorph body type to lose fat and maintain weight when they follow a healthy diet and exercise program. Mesomorphs are more muscular than the endomorph or ectomorph body types.

Mesomorph metabolism is faster than the metabolism of the endomorph body type but slower than the metabolism of an ectomorph. It is easy for people with a mesomorph body type to lose excess weight when they follow a low-fat, high-protein eating plan with the proper number of calories and plenty of exercise. Mesomorphs gain weight quickly if their eating plans contain too many calories from high-fat, high-sugar foods. As mesomorphs age, they will need to follow a strict plan of diet and exercise to maintain their muscle mass and fitness level. Mesomorphs must be sure not to take their body type for granted or they will become fat and unfit.

Muscle building comes very easily to people with a mesomorph body type. This might be one of the reasons why so many professional athletes have this build. Even an out-of-shape mesomorph who wants to get back into shape will quickly change flabby muscles to fit, well-defined muscles with relative ease. Mesomorphs are solidly built and well-suited to activities that require strength and endurance, such as swimming and hiking.

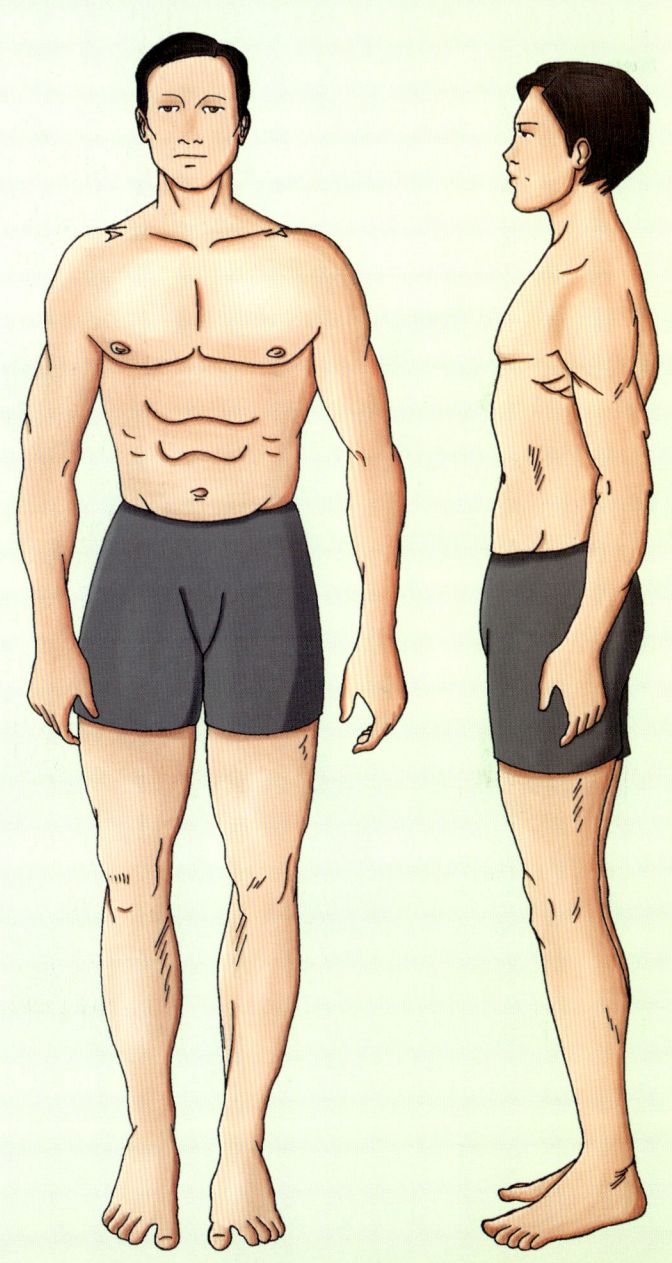

## Astonishing fact

There are 15,000 different kinds of rice!

DIET AND RECIPES

## Endomorph body type diet

The characteristics of an endomorph body type include a rounder body with a waist that is often bigger than the chest. Endomorph body types often have short arms and legs, with the upper part of the limbs being larger than the lower part. People with this body type tend to store fat easily and have more difficulty losing weight.

The endomorph body type maybe the hardest body type to have in terms of managing weight and overall fitness. The ectomorph body type usually describes people who are tall and skinny. The mesomorph body type describes people with an athletic body. A person with an endomorph body type usually has a slow metabolism. They eat small amounts of food and still tend to gain weight. Excess calories can turn into fat quickly for someone with an endomorph body type. It is possible for endomorphs to lose weight, but it can sometimes be a slow process.

Those with an endomorph body type need to stay on a strict diet in order to maintain a healthy weight and lifestyle. This body type does not process carbohydrates well. Endomorphs should eat a diet of low carbohydrates and consume plenty of protein. Protein can help people with this body type gain muscle and burn fat.

Eating meals that are lower in fat will also help people with an endomorph body type. Some believe that endomorphs have more fat cells in the body than other body types. Low-fat meals and snacks will decrease the chance of creating more fat cells in the body. A low-fat diet should be filled with healthy foods such as lean meats, fruits and vegetables.

### Astonishing fact

Rice is the chief food for half the people of the world.

# Some healthy recipes

## Buckwheat buttermilk pancakes

### Ingredients

- 1 cup flour
- ½ teaspoon salt
- 1 teaspoon baking powder
- 1 teaspoon baking soda
- 2 tablespoons sugar
- 1 cup buckwheat flour
- 1 egg, well beaten
- ¼ cup butter, melted (or ¼ c. salad oil)
- 2 cups buttermilk

### Method

Into a medium bowl, mix flour with salt, baking powder, baking soda and sugar. Stir in buckwheat flour. Set aside.

In another small bowl mix egg, butter and buttermilk well. Add to the flour mixture, mixing only until combined (will be lumpy).

In the meantime, slowly heat a griddle or frying pan. Use 1/4 cup batter for each pancake. Cook until bubbles form on surface and edges become dry. Turn; cook for 2 minutes longer or until nicely browned on underside. Serve warm, with butter and maple syrup.

### Astonishing fact

After the 'Popeye' comic strip started in 1931; spinach consumption went up by thirty-three per cent in the United States!

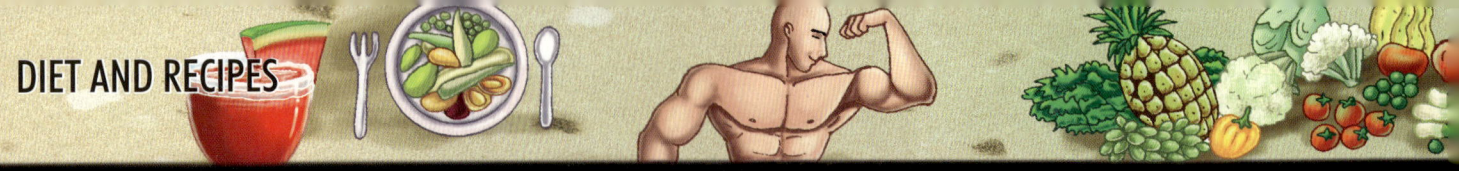

DIET AND RECIPES

## Western omelette

### Ingredients

- 1/2 cup egg substitute
- 1/2 cup potatoes, diced
- 1/4 cup of finely chopped green peppers
- 1/4 cup of finely chopped red peppers
- 1/4 cup of finely chopped onions
- 1 teaspoon light margarine

## Method

In a non-stick frying pan, over medium heat, fry potatoes, peppers and onions in 1-teaspoon light margarine until tender. Remove from frying pan; keep warm.

Pour egg substitute into frying pan. Cook lifting edges to allow uncooked portion to flow underneath.

When almost set, spoon vegetable mixture over half of the omelette. Fold other half over vegetable mixture; slide onto serving plate.

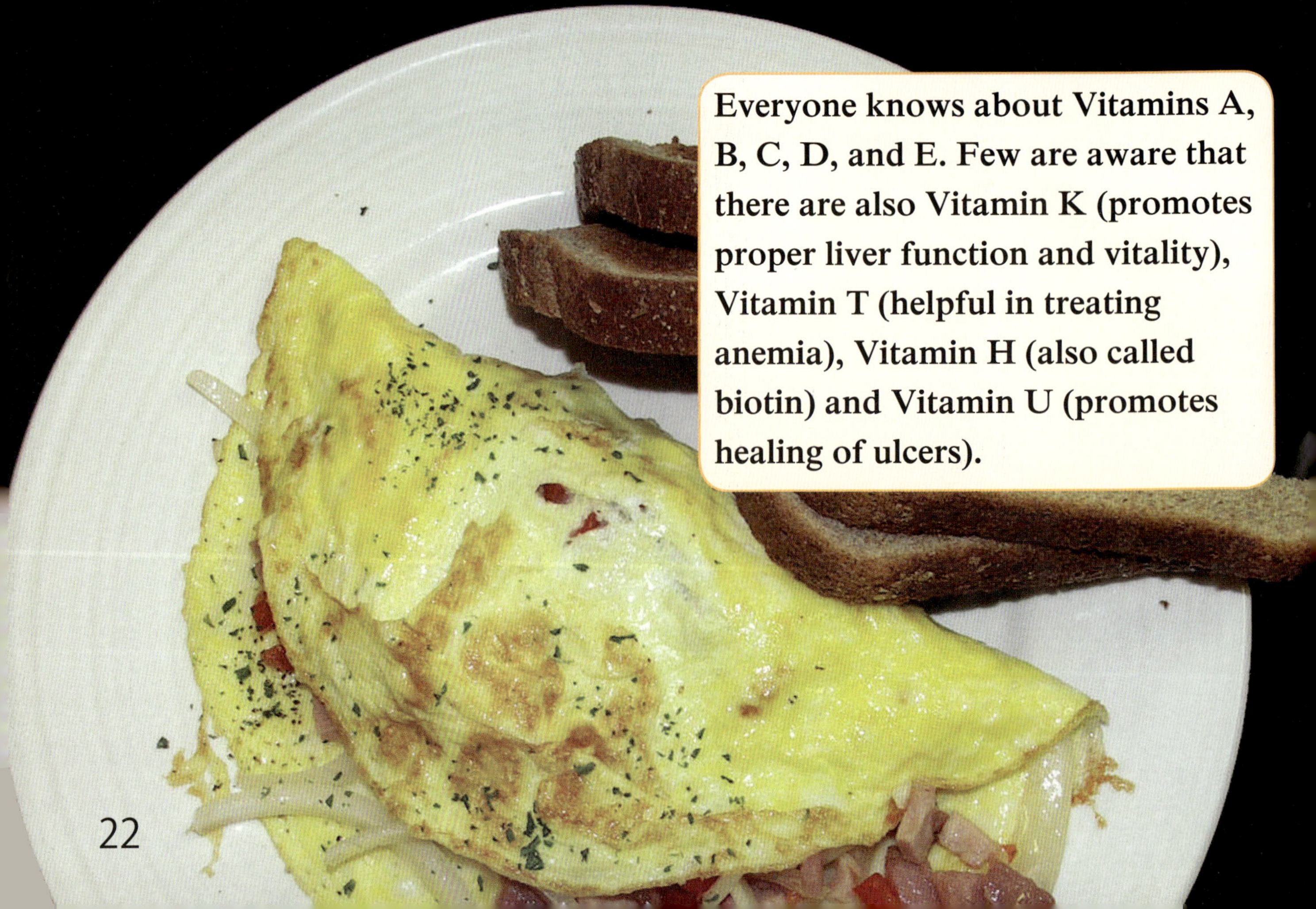

> Everyone knows about Vitamins A, B, C, D, and E. Few are aware that there are also Vitamin K (promotes proper liver function and vitality), Vitamin T (helpful in treating anemia), Vitamin H (also called biotin) and Vitamin U (promotes healing of ulcers).

# Some healthy recipes

## Chicken soup

**Ingredients**

- 250 grams breast of chicken
- Cabbage
- 1 carrot
- 3-4 french beans
- 1 capsicum
- 1 onion
- 2-3 cloves of garlic
- Black pepper
- Corn flour
- salt

## Method

Chop chicken into small pieces. Mince garlic and chop onion. Grate cabbage. Chop carrot, capsicum and French beans. Grind black pepper.

In a pot, put chicken and water. Add minced garlic, salt and onion. Boil them in a low flame. When the chicken pieces are fully boiled, add all the vegetables and cook again for five minutes.

Take the corn flour and then mix it in cold water. Mix that in the soup and put to boil. The amount of corn flour will decide the consistency of the soup. The thicker you want, the more will be the amount. Serve your soup hot along with bread and butter.

### Astonishing fact

**In ancient Rome it was considered a sin to eat the flesh of a Woodpecker.**

# DIET AND RECIPES

## Astonishing fact

French fries are actually made in huge factories, frozen, and then processed. The oils and fats are highly processed and highly fatty.

## Low-fat grilled chicken salad

### Ingredients

- Boneless, skinless chicken breast: 400g
- Potatoes: 300g (cut in half)
- Green beans: 200g
- Orange marmalade: 2 tablespoons
- Leaf lettuce: 3 cups (torn)
- Oranges: 2 (peeled and sectioned)
- Orange juice: 1/4 cup
- Salt and black pepper: Add to taste
- Diced ginger: 1/2 teaspoon

### Method

Mix orange juice, marmalade, salt, pepper, orange peel and ginger. Take about 1/4 cup and brush on to the chicken. Then grill until both sides browned. Cut the chicken into slices.

Boil the potatoes for 8 to 10 minutes until tender. Also boil the green beans for 2 to 3 minutes until cooked. Then drain the water.

In a large salad bowl, mix the chicken, orange slices, potatoes and green beans.

Some healthy recipes

# Irish chicken stew with dumplings

### Ingredients

- 2 cans condensed cream of chicken soup
- 3 cups water
- 1 cup chopped celery
- 2 onions, quartered
- 1 teaspoon salt
- 1/2 teaspoon poultry seasoning
- 1/2 teaspoon ground black pepper
- 4 skinless, boneless chicken breast halves
- 5 carrots, sliced
- 1 package frozen green peas
- 4 potatoes, quartered
- 3 cups baking mix
- 1-1/3 cups milk

> With all the processing that the fast food goes through during manufacturing, a lot of essential nutrients go missing. Fibres, vitamins and minerals get destroyed during this process and what it leaves for you is just unhealthy fats and empty calories.

## Method

In a large, heavy pot, combine soup, water, chicken, celery, onion, salt, poultry seasoning and pepper. Cover and cook over low heat for about 1-1/2 hours.

Add potatoes and carrots; cover and cook another 30 minutes.

Remove chicken from pot, shred it and return to the pot. Add peas and cook only 5 minutes longer.

Add dumplings. To make dumplings: Mix baking mix and milk until a soft dough forms. Drop by tablespoonfuls into boiling stew. Cover it for 10 minutes on a low flame, then uncover and simmer for another additional 10 minutes.

# DIET AND RECIPES

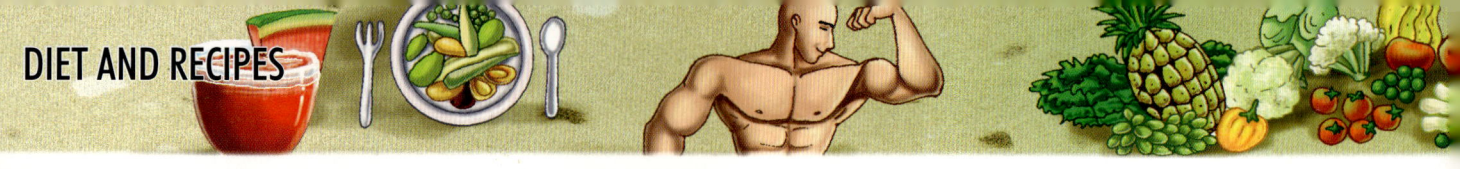

## Spicy baked chicken casserole with peppers, chickpeas and rice

### Ingredients

- 1 tbsp Olive oil
- 8 Chicken pieces (thighs and drumsticks)
- 2 Yellow peppers, sliced
- 2 Onions, sliced
- 1 bunch Cilantro
- 3 cloves Garlic
- 1-2 Green chilies
- 1/2 cup canned chickpeas
- 1 cup Basmati rice
- 1 Large lemon
- 3/4 cup Pitted green olives
- 1 1/4 cup Chicken stock

## Method

Place a large casserole to heat in the oven. Heat 1 tbsp olive oil in a large frying pan and brown 8 chicken pieces (thighs and drumsticks) all over.

Remove from pan, increase heat and cook 2 sliced yellow peppers and 2 sliced onions until well-browned at the edges.

Add 1 bunch fresh coriander (cilantro), washed and chopped, 3 cloves crushed garlic, 1-2 green chillies, halved, seeded and finely chopped, 3 tsp ground coriander seeds, 100g (1/2 cup) chick peas, 175g (1 cup) basmati rice. Stir well.

Pour in the juice of 1 large lemon and 275ml (1 ¼ cups) chicken stock and bring to boil. Carefully pour this mixture into the pre-heated casserole.

Stir in 100g (3/4 cup) pitted green olives.

Place the chicken pieces on top, cover and bake for 50-60 minutes until the rice is cooked.

### Astonishing fact

If you want to lose weight, choose low-fat dairy products – aim for three servings each day such as a glass of skimmed milk, 1 small pot of low-fat yoghurt and a matchbox-sized piece of reduced-fat cheese.

# Some healthy recipes

## Brownies

### Ingredients

- Unsweetened chocolate: 100g
- Flour: 1 cup
- Walnuts: 1/2 cup
- Soy margarine: 1 cup
- Maple sugar: 1 1/2 cup
- Eggs: 4
- Salt: 1/2 teaspoon
- Vanilla extract: 1 tbsp

## Method

Pre-heat the oven to 325 degrees.

On low heat, melt and mix chocolate and margarine. Let it cool.

Mix sugar, eggs and vanilla. Whisk until frothy, and add the chocolate mixture.

Add in flour, salt, walnuts and mix well.

Place in a lightly greased pan, and bake for 25 to 30 minutes.

## Astonishing fact

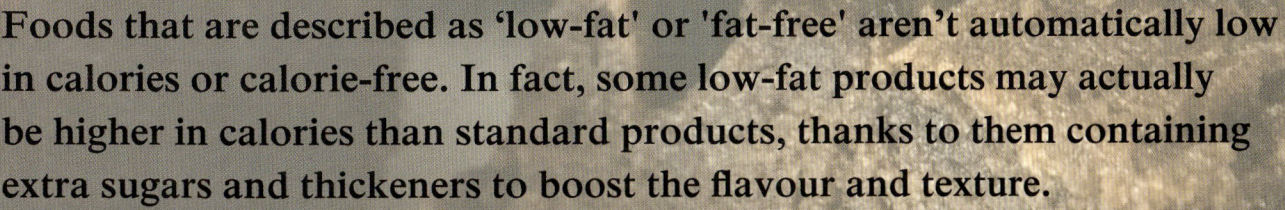

Foods that are described as 'low-fat' or 'fat-free' aren't automatically low in calories or calorie-free. In fact, some low-fat products may actually be higher in calories than standard products, thanks to them containing extra sugars and thickeners to boost the flavour and texture.

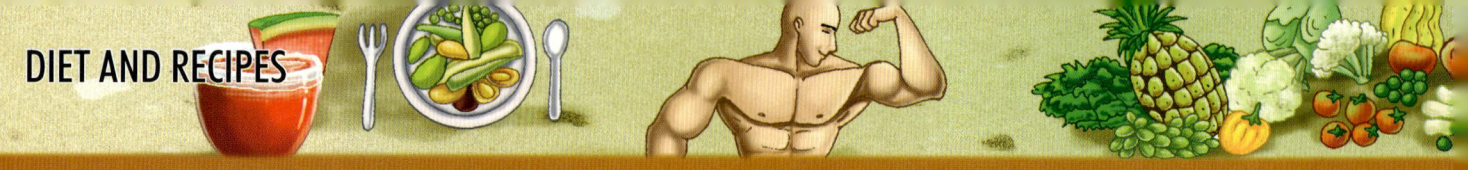

# DIET AND RECIPES

## Sugar-free muffin

### Ingredients

- 1 stick butter
- 3 eggs
- 1 cup pineapple juice
- 1 teaspoon lemon juice
- 2 ½ cups flour
- 1 teaspoon baking soda
- 2 teaspoons baking powder
- ½ teaspoon salt
- 1 cup well-drained crushed pineapple

### Method

Preheat oven to 180 degree Celsius.

Combine the butter and eggs in a mixing bowl and beat until the mixture is light and smooth. Add the pineapple juice and lemon juice and mix well. In another smaller bowl, mix together the flour, baking soda, baking powder and salt. Add the flour mixture to the butter and eggs. Mix well. Stir in the crushed pineapple. Do not over mix the batter as it will result in a tough muffin.

Grease a 12-hole muffin tin or line with paper muffin cups. Fill the cups two-thirds full with the muffin mix. Bake for 20 minutes or until a toothpick inserted into the muffins comes out clean.

### Astonishing fact

In ancient China and certain parts of India, mouse flesh was considered a great delicacy. In ancient Greece, where the mouse was sacred to Apollo, mice were sometimes devoured by temple priests.

Some healthy recipes

## Tuna mixed vegetable pasta

### Ingredients

- Tuna can: 200g (drained)
- Mushrooms: 1 1/2 cup (sliced)
- Tomato paste: 1 tablespoon
- Tomato juice: 1 1/4 cup
- Pasta shapes: 350g
- Green onions: 5 (sliced diagonally)
- Grounded peppercorns: 1 teaspoon
- Frozen peas: 1 cup
- Red pepper: 1/2 (seeded and chopped)
- Garlic: 1 clove (crushed)
- Olive oil: 2 tablespoon

## Method

Heat the oil in a pan and add mushrooms, garlic and pepper. Cook until mushrooms are soft.

Add in tomato paste, tomato juice and peas. Bring to boil. Then lower the heat and simmer.

Cook the pasta according to package directions. When the pasta is almost done, add the tuna to the sauce and heat gently and add in green onions.

Drain the pasta and serve with the sauce.

### Astonishing fact

Half the foods eaten throughout the world today were developed by farmers in the Andes Mountains. Potatoes, maize, sweet potatoes, squash, all varieties of beans, peanuts, manioc, cashews, pineapples, chocolate, avocados, tomatoes, peppers, papayas, strawberries, mulberries and many other foods were first grown in this region.

DIET AND RECIPES

## Citrus fruit smoothie

### Ingredients

- 5 cups grapefruit juice
- 3 cups orange juice
- 1 cup water
- 4 medium firm bananas, cut up and frozen
- 12 frozen unsweetened strawberries

## Methods

In a blender, place half of each ingredient; cover and process until smooth.

Pour into a pitcher.

Repeat.

Serve immediately.

## Watermelon juice

### Ingredients

- 2 cups chopped seeded watermelon
- 1 cup crushed ice
- 2 teaspoons honey
- 1/4 teaspoon black pepper
- fresh mint

## Method

Combine watermelon, ice, honey and black pepper in a blender.

Blend until smooth.

Garnish with mint.

Serve chilled.

Stir well before serving.

### Astonishing fact

The staple food of the Kanembu, a tribe living on the shores of Lake Chad in Africa, is Algae. The Kanembu harvest a common variety known as Spirulina from the lake, dry it on the sand, mix it up into a spicy cake, and eat it with tomatoes and chilli peppers.

# Test Your MEMORY

1. What is diet?

2. What do you understand by a balanced diet?

3. What are the different types of diet?

4. What is the Body Mass Index?

5. Write about the importance of diet in your life.

6. Write about the role of carbohydrates in your diet.

7. Are fats important in your diet?

8. Write about the role fibres play in your diet.

9. Write about the importance of water in your diet.

10. Write the diet recommended for an ectomorphic body.

11. Write the diet recommended for a mesomorphic body.

12. Write the diet recommended for an endomorphic body.

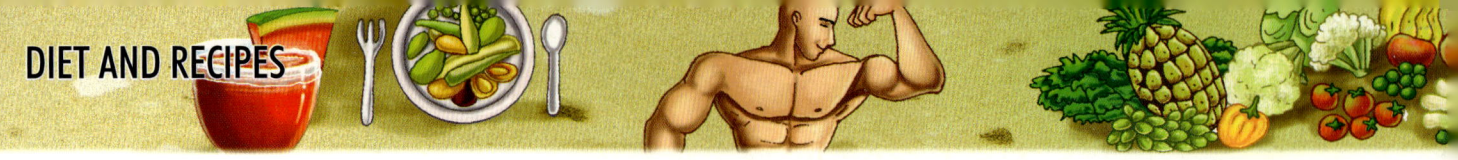

# Index

### A
Adolphe Quetelet 11

### B
balanced diet 3, 4, 5, 13, 14
Body mass index (BMI) 11

### C
calories 4, 7, 9, 10, 18, 19, 20, 25, 27
carbohydrates 5, 10, 15, 18, 20

### E
ectomorph 18, 19, 20
endomorph 18, 19, 20
exchange-type diet 7

### F
fats 5, 15, 16, 18, 24, 25
fibre 5, 10
fixed-menu diet 7
flexible diets 9
formula diets 8

### G
glucose 15

### L
low-calorie diet 10
low-fat diet 10, 20

### M
mesomorph 18, 19, 20
minerals 4, 5, 17, 25

### N
nutrients 3, 4, 5, 13, 14, 15, 16, 17, 25

### P
pre-packaged meal diet 8
proteins 5, 15, 18

### Q
Quetelet Index 11

### S
starch 7, 15
sucrose 15

### V
vitamins 4, 5, 16, 22, 25

### W
water 4, 17, 22, 24, 25, 30